ZERO MOSTEL'S BOOK OF VILLAINS

Zero Mostel's Book of Villains

by Zero Mostel
with Israel Shenker

photographed by
Alex Gotfryd

Doubleday and Company, Inc.
Garden City, New York 1976

792
M

AN EXCULPATING PREFACE

Over the ages, multitudes of callous sinners and
hardened culprits have been condemned without
mercy, punished without relief, imprisoned without parole,
even executed.

The task to which this book is dedicated is to review the
harshness of the past and renew the memory of the
miscreants who have offended against humanity and
the law. We then can re-examine our attitudes toward the
miscreants of our own day and perhaps revise our
standards of punishment and pardon.

To document each case, Zero Mostel represents the
villain and Israel Shenker states the crime.

Alex Gotfryd has taken the pictures from A to Zero.

THE ROSTER

Adam and Eve and the Serpent
Benedict Arnold
Alexander Graham Bell
Bluebeard
John Wilkes Booth
Lucrezia Borgia
Brutus
Cain
Al Capone
Delilah
Lord Elgin
Albert Bacon Fall
Frankenstein
George III
Henry VIII
Jack the Ripper
Dr. Jekyll and Mr. Hyde
Jezebel
The Knave of Hearts
The Loch Ness Monster
Lady Macbeth

Marie Antoinette
Mata Hari
Medea
Medusa
Multinational Corporations:
    Attila the Hun
    Genghis Khan
    Ivan the Terrible
Napoleon
Nebuchadnezzer
Nero
Pharaoh
Rasputin
Robespierre
Marquis de Sade
Salome
Satan
Boss Tweed
The Wolf
Zero Mostel

ZERO MOSTEL'S BOOK OF VILLAINS

ADAM and EVE and the SERPENT. The Serpent was the subtlest animal God created, and he persuaded Eve to eat the fruit of the tree of knowledge.

Then Eve persuaded Adam—

and that's how all the trouble started. But an apple a day does keep the doctor away. And the Serpent has been crawling on his belly and biting the dust long enough.

BENEDICT ARNOLD (1741–1801) was an energetic and successful American general during the Revolutionary War. Despite George Washington's backing, Arnold was passed over while others were promoted to major general. But Arnold was such a good military man that he finally got his promotion and played a major role in leading his troops to victory. In 1780 he took command of West Point and decided to surrender it to the British in exchange for money and a commission in the British Army. When the plot was discovered, Arnold escaped. Turning his coat, he got his new commission, promptly attacked Virginia, and burned Richmond.

ALEXANDER GRAHAM BELL (1847–1922) invented the
telephone, and also the first recording surfaces—for
phonographs. He is not responsible for busy signals
or rock music. Besides, once he realized his mistakes,
he moved to Nova Scotia and flew a kite—the
tetrahedral one he invented.

BLUEBEARD is the nickname of the chevalier Raoul in a story by Charles Perrault. When Bluebeard's seventh wife opened a locked door and discovered the remains of her six predecessors, Bluebeard was ready to make short shrift of her. But she was saved by her brothers, who arrived just in time. Bluebeard has also been identified as Gilles de Rais (1404–40), a French marshal who is said to have kept the bodies of his murdered wives all in one room.

JOHN WILKES BOOTH (1838–65) made his debut as an actor and egomaniac at age seventeen. in Baltimore. He won plaudits for Shakespearean roles but was never content with the size of the headlines, so he decided to kidnap Abraham Lincoln. When that plot failed, he went to Ford's Theater, in Washington, entered the presidential box, and shot Lincoln. After a two-week hunt, Booth was tracked down and killed — either by his own hand or by that of a pursuer.

LUCREZIA BORGIA (1480–1519) was brought up with every advantage: her father was Pope Alexander VI, and her brother was the celebrated poisoner Cesare Borgia, who instructed her in the family trade and taught her never to leave poison in the cups. She married three times, and loved to sit at home twiddling her rings.

BRUTUS (c. 85–42 B.C.) was a Roman official, extortionate, cruel, stubborn, and treacherous. Though Caesar forgave him for siding with an enemy cause, Brutus nonetheless joined Cassius in another plot against Caesar. When Caesar was assassinated, Brutus took the side of the republicans and held power in Macedonia. In a battle for control, Brutus was on the losing side, and he committed suicide.

CAIN, eldest son of Adam and Eve, was a tiller of the soil and the first murderer. In a jealous rage, he killed his brother Abel with the jawbone of an ass, reducing the population to three. When he tried to flee, God found him.

AL CAPONE (1899–1947) was born in Naples, educated in New York, and nailed in Chicago for not paying his income tax. Serving first as lieutenant to a crime boss, then as his own head man, Alfonso (or Alphonse) Capone ran speakeasies, gambling, shakedowns, music, and other murderous vices. His crime syndicate terrorized Chicago in the 1920s, and the Federal Bureau of Internal Revenue estimated that he collected $105 million in 1927 alone.

DELILAH was a courtesan on the payroll of the Philistines. Discovering that the strength of her lover, Samson, was in his long hair, she betrayed him to his enemies by cutting it off.

LORD ELGIN (1766–1841) was the 7th Earl of Elgin, and he served his sovereign on diplomatic missions to Vienna, Brussels, Berlin, and Constantinople. All this is buried in the archives. What is out in the open is a side trip to Greece which allowed Lord Elgin to whisk the so-called Elgin marbles out of Athens, where they belonged, to England, where they didn't belong.

ALBERT BACON FALL (1861–1944) was a rancher in the Southwest who went into politics. After serving in the U. S. Senate, he was named Secretary of the Interior by President Harding. Fall leased the Teapot Dome oil fields without competitive bidding, and the resulting Teapot Dome scandal rocked Harding's administration and the Republican Party. Fall resigned in 1923 and was put on trial. In 1931 he was convicted of conspiracy to defraud the government.

FRANKENSTEIN is the title of a horror story by Mary Wollstonecraft Shelley. She wrote of a German student — Frankenstein — who learned how to make a monster out of odds and ends lying about the lab, and who then brought the fellow to life. The monster murdered Frankenstein's bride, family, and friends. Frankenstein died of grief, and the monster — who only wanted to be loved — was full of second thoughts and worries about the verdict of history.

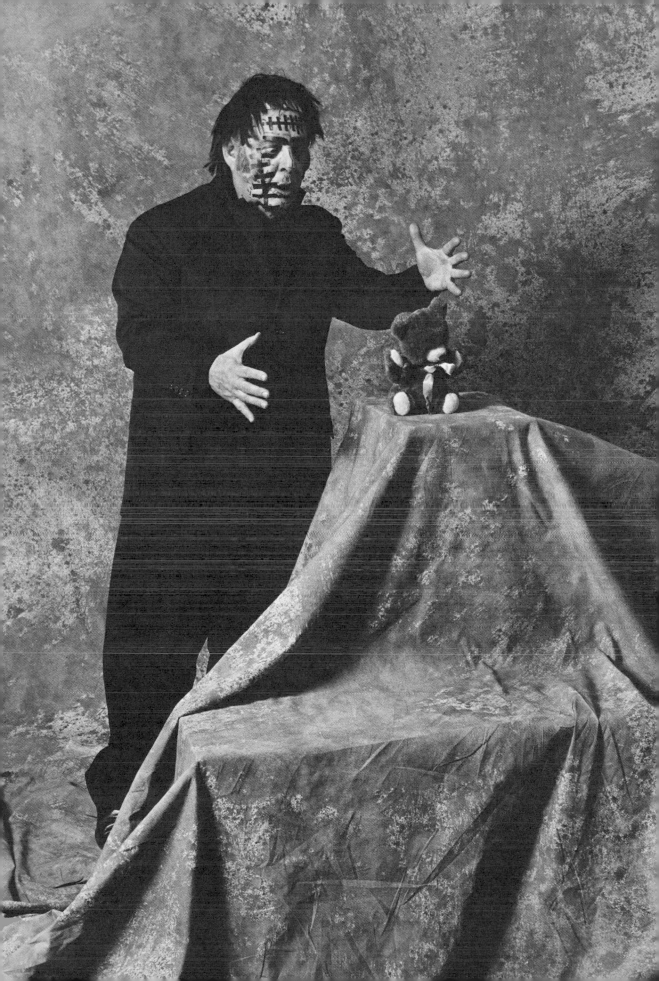

GEORGE III (1738–1820) was dominated by his mother and the Earl of Bute. He was stubborn, not terribly bright, and intolerant of dissent. He believed in taxation without representation, and tried to make his American subjects pay a tax for tea. The colonists revolted and declared themselves independent, which meant the beginning of the end for the British Empire. George suffered fits of insanity, and finally lost his reason completely.

HENRY VIII (1491–1547) was a skilled musician, an inveterate plotter, an unabashed egotist, and a recidivist groom. He had six wives, and showed a penchant for divorcing them or having them beheaded. One result was a break with Rome.

JACK THE RIPPER was a single-minded nineteenth-century killer who chose his victims among London's prostitutes, and always slipped through the police net. It was widely believed that he was a member of the Royal Family, benefiting from official complicity.

DR. JEKYLL and MR. HYDE were the inseparable characters in a story by Robert Louis Stevenson. Dr. Jekyll invented a potion which turned him into —

Mr. Hyde, the incarnation of Jekyll's own evil desires. Eventually Hyde committed a murder, got the upper hand with Jekyll, and then killed themselves. Hyde, of course, was not really himself half the time.

JEZEBEL (d.c. 846 B.C.) was a Phoenician princess who encouraged idolatry, persecuted the prophets, and mercilessly hounded Elijah. But the prophet Elijah gave Jezebel the willies by accurately prophesying her doom.

THE KNAVE OF HEARTS, he stole the tarts which the Queen of Hearts had baked, all on a summer's day.

THE LOCH NESS MONSTER, fifty feet long and sinuous, has been sighted innumerable times, but he has never been seen. He lurks at the bottom of dark Scottish waters, resisting scientific probes and the man from Loch Lomond who wants him to move there.

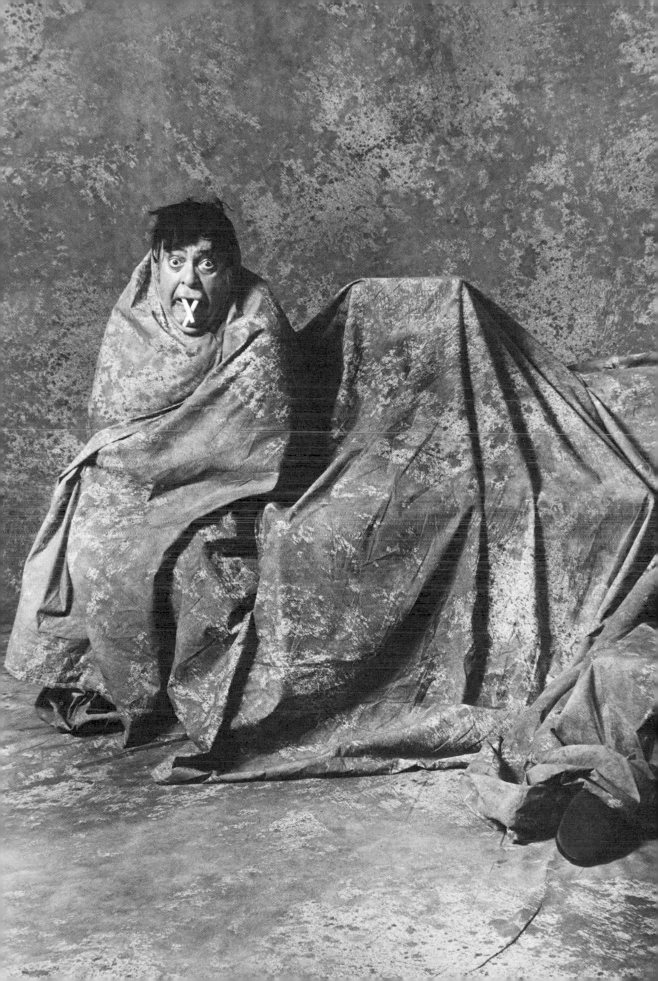

LADY MACBETH, in a play by Shakespeare, was a scheming wife, and she kept nagging her husband to kill King Duncan. When Macbeth's nerve failed, Lady Macbeth killed Duncan's servants, and she was almost caught red-handed. There was a real Macbeth (d. 1057) who was King of Scotland, and who fought and killed Duncan I. He was a male chauvinist who would not let his wife get away with murder.

MARIE ANTOINETTE (1755–93) was the daughter of Maria Theresa and Francis I of Austria, and she became the French queen, wife of Louis XVI. But her husband kept to himself, and she was very unhappy. Came the Revolution and she and Louis fled from Paris. They were seized by the rebels and subjected to the highest form of lèse majesté. When she was told — in the halcyon days before the rabble took over — that the people had no bread, she is supposed to have said, "Let them eat cake." Despite her epigrammatic facility, she was tried by a Revolutionary Tribunal, condemned, and guillotined.

MATA HARI (1876–1917) was a Dutch dancer who spied for the Germans during World War I, betraying the secrets she picked up from the many Allied officers with whom she was intimate. She was executed by the French.

MEDEA, a princess in Greek mythology, was expert at magic. When she fell in love with Jason, she helped him get the Golden Fleece and then fled with him, chopping her brother into pieces and scattering them in the path of her father, who was in hot pursuit. Medea then lived with Jason as his wife, and when Jason tried to flee from her to marry someone else, Medea provided an enchanted wedding gown which burned her rival to death. She also killed her own children.

MEDUSA was one of the three Gorgon monster-sisters in Greek mythology. She started off beautiful, but when she offended Athena her hair was changed to snakes, and she became so hideous that anybody who looked at her was changed to stone. But Medusa spent hours looking at herself in the mirror without turning a hair. Even after she died, her head was petrifying to behold.

ATTILA THE HUN (c. 406–53) was called the Scourge of God. He began by sharing power over the Huns with his brother, and then he murdered his brother. For years he extorted tribute from the Eastern Roman Emperor, and then he pillaged the Emperor's lands, proving absolutely savage with people who cheated on their income tributes. His patience was once more tried when his request for half of the Western Empire, as a dowry, was refused. Attila's army was finally defeated in Gaul, and then it was laid even lower by short provisions and devastating disease. Attila himself died of nosebleed while celebrating one of his own weddings.

MULTINATIONAL CORPORATION 2 — GK

GENGHIS KHAN (c. 1162–1227) was a Mongol chief who fought his way to the top of a Mongol union. Then he conquered big.chunks of China and neighboring territories, extending his carnage and his rule to one of the greatest empires ever known. He died with his helmet on, but some historians suggest that he did not fight fair. It is true that he destroyed whole cities, spread a reign of terror, and used prisoners as a shield in attacks. He also took all the credit.

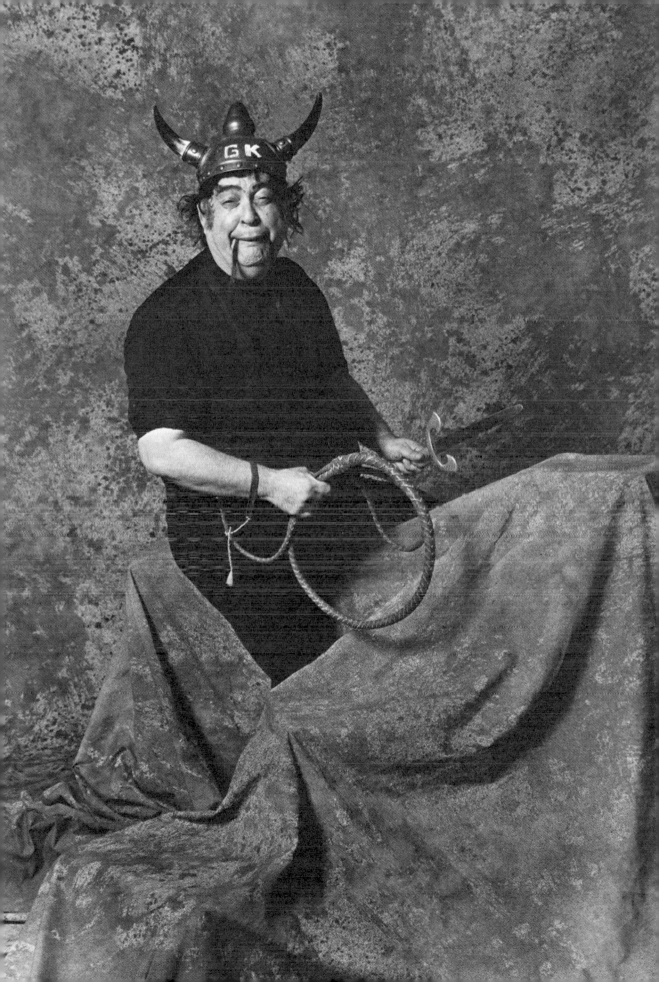

MULTINATIONAL CORPORATION 3 — ITT

IVAN THE TERRIBLE (1530–84) was haughty, gloomy, cruel — in fact, terrible. He was the first man to be called Czar, and he ruled with consuming savagery. Ivan killed his eldest son, married seven times, forced his unwanted wives to become nuns, and was nasty to the back-room boyars (nobles).

NAPOLEON (1769–1821), because of his size, was known at school as "the little Corporal." He was a gifted military leader, not averse to using what he called "a whiff of grapeshot" for dispersing mobs, and all of French manhood to realize his ambitions for conquest. He invaded countries all over the map, and gave many of them to his relatives. Napoleon caused great bitterness by rising from little corporal to big Emperor without going to West Point.

NEBUCHADNEZZER (c. 605–562 B.C.) killed all the nobles of Judah, destroyed the art work in the Lord's temple, and—as the Bible says—"carried away all Jerusalem." This included 10,000 captives plus the king's mother and the king's wives. He decreed that all who heard the horn, pipe, lyre, harp, or bagpipe should fall down and worship a golden image. N. smote his enemies, and had Shadrach, Meshach, and Abednego cast into a fiery furnace. He ate grass like an ox and let his hair grow long as eagle's feathers, and his nails were like bird's claws. But the Bible never did know whether to spell his name Nabuchadrezzar, Nebuchadrezzar, Nebuchadnezzar, or Nebuchodonosor. Modern scholars found that it was really Nabukudurruusur. With such a crisis of identity, no wonder he chewed grass.

NERO (37–68) fiddled while Rome burned, and he was even charged with setting the fire. Rumor had it that Nero wanted a fiery backdrop for his recitation on the fall of Troy. When the fire died down, he rebuilt Rome magnificently, laying out great streets and building a grand palace. He was licentious, played with matches, murdered his rivals and even his mother and his wife, and forced people to listen to his concerts. Just before committing suicide, he said modestly, "What an artist the world is losing in me!"

PHARAOH enslaved the Israelites and ordered the slaughter of their male children. Actually, Pharaoh is the title of the ancient kings of Egypt; the Pharaoh who subjugated the Jews was probably Seti I, and his son Ramses II was the Pharaoh who pursued the Jews during their exodus from Egypt.

GRIGORY YEFIMOVICH RASPUTIN (c. 1872–1916) was a
semiliterate Russian monk of hypnotic appearance who
encouraged orgies, had a baleful influence at the Czar's
court, and corrupted the Russian Orthodox Church. He
gained an ascendance over the Czarina by an apparent
ability to check the bleeding of her son, who suffered
from hemophilia. Those who opposed Rasputin were cast
from office and replaced by people who were corrupt
and incompetent. But he kept himself fit: after his assassins
failed to kill him with potassium cyanide, they were
reduced to shooting him dead and drowning him for
good measure. His corpse was later exhumed and
burned.

MAXIMILIEN MARIE ISIDORE ROBESPIERRE (1758–94) was a poor youth who studied law on a scholarship, won plaudits for his skill and dedication, and became a prominent member of French Revolutionary assemblies. He insisted on the execution of the French King, and then presided over the Reign of Terror, using the guillotine to kill his enemies. Robespierre founded a civic religion, and when he seemed determined to keep on purging sinners he was overthrown, arrested, tried, and guillotined, leaving the Reign of Terror without a head.

MARQUIS DE SADE (1740–1814) was a French author famous for daring novels and not-so-daring essays. For conduct considered scandalous he was imprisoned, and then reimprisoned for writings considered scandalous. De Sade suggested that because sexual deviation and crimes existed they were natural. Naturally, he wrote bestsellers. He enriched the language with the word sadism.

SALOME, using seven veils, danced seductively for her
stepfather Herod, and asked for the head of John the
Baptist on a platter. He fulfilled her wish, giving her
the head and the Bible one of its less pleasing images.

SATAN was originally a good angel, and decided of his own free will to be bad, thus turning into a fallen angel and dragging other angels down with him. These devils tempted men and accounted for evil in the world. Satan really wanted his independence from God, as well as a smidgen of equality. In the Middle Ages, folk tales ascribed to Satan hoofs, horns, suave manners, and sulphurous breath. All along, he operated under a lot of aliases, such as Evil One, Prince of Darkness, Lucifer, and Beelzebub.